Oxford Read and Discover

2

Jobs

Kamini Khanduri

Contents

OXFORD

UNIVERSITY PRESS

OXFORD
UNIVERSITY PRESS

Great Clarendon Street, Oxford, OX2 6DP, United Kingdom

Oxford University Press is a department of the University of Oxford. It furthers the University's objective of excellence in research, scholarship, and education by publishing worldwide. Oxford is a registered trade mark of Oxford University Press in the UK and in certain other countries

ISBN: 978 0 19 464686 4

An Audio CD Pack containing this book and a CD is also available, ISBN 978 0 19 464696 3

The CD has a choice of American and British English recordings of the complete text.

An accompanying Activity Book is also available, ISBN 978 0 19 464676 5

Printed in China

This book is printed on paper from certified and well-managed sources.

ACKNOWLEDGEMENTS

Illustrations by: Kelly Kennedy pp.5; Alan Rowe pp.20, 22, 24, 26, 28, 30, 32, 34, 38, 39.

The Publishers would also like to thank the following for their kind permission to reproduce photographs and other copyright material: Alamy pp.3 (bus driver/Charles Bowman, farmer/Warren Jacobs/Art Directors), 5 (David R. Frazier Photolibrary, Inc), 6 (chef/ Alissa Everett, tour guide/Jason Lindsey), 7 (Charles Bowman), 8 (farmer/Warren Jacobs/Art Directors, olive seller/Simon Tilley), 9 (fishermen/RIA Novosti), 12 (teacher/AfriPics.com), 13 (Imagebroker), 17 (railway workers/Qaphotos.com), 19 (musicians/ Fotomaton, making a movie/Shoosmith Bollywood Collection); Corbis pp.3 (doctor/JLP/Jose L. Pelaez), 9 (miner/Gideon Mendel), 12 (doctor/JLP/Jose L. Pelaez), 15 (washing a pelican/Julie Dermansky), 16 (Fan Xia/Xinhua Press); Getty Images pp.4 (road builders/Gallo Images), 10 (potter/Tim Graham), 14 (China Photos/Stringer), 17 (taxi driver/Karl Johaentges/LOOK), 18 (Getty Images/Stringer); Oxford University Press pp.3 (teacher), 4 (office), 11, 17 (taxi drivers); Science Photo Library p.10 (ice-cream factory/Massimo Brega, The Lighthouse), 15 (guide dog training/Pierre Philippon/Look at Sciences).

 # Introduction

What is a job? A job is the work that you do. A teacher does a job. A bus driver does a job, too. Most people do jobs for money, but not all jobs are for money.

What does a doctor do?
Where does a farmer work?
What jobs do you know?

 Now read and discover more about jobs!

1 Jobs

Some jobs are inside. These people are working in an office. They are using telephones and computers.

Some jobs are outside. These people are making a new road. They have orange clothes so other people can see them.

Making a Road

flight attendants

passengers

On a Plane

Some people work in the same place every day. Some people go to lots of places. Flight attendants work on planes. They help the passengers. Flight attendants wear a uniform so passengers can find them.

Discover!

Firefighters wear a uniform to protect their body. They can go into very, very hot buildings!

→ Go to pages 20–21 for activities.

2 In the City

Cities are big and busy. Lots of people work in cities. People work in stores, parks, and libraries.

Chefs work in restaurants. They cook the food.

Many tourists go to cities. Tour guides work with tourists. They help tourists to learn about a city.

Chefs

A Tour Guide

A Bus Driver

When you are in a city, how can you go from a park to a library? Maybe you take a bus or a train. Bus drivers and train drivers are doing a job. In cities, there are lots of jobs for drivers.

→ Go to pages 22–23 for activities.

3 In the Countryside

A Farmer

In the countryside, many jobs are outside. Farmers work in the countryside. Some farmers keep animals, and some farmers grow crops. Rice, bananas, and olives are crops.

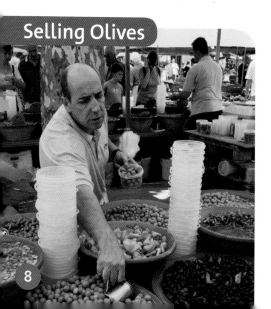

Selling Olives

Some farmers sell their animals or crops at a market. Some farmers sell their animals or crops to a store. That's how farmers make money.

boat

Catching Fish

Some people catch fish and sell them. They go in boats to catch fish from the ocean.

Miners work in mines under the ground. Their job is to find coal, metal, or other things.

A Gold Miner

Discover!

Some gold mines are more than 3 kilometers under the ground!

Go to pages 24–25 for activities.

Making Things

What other jobs are there? Lots of people make things. People use their hands to make some things. This man is making a pot.

Many people work in factories. They use machines to make things. This woman is making ice creams.

Making a Pot

Making Ice Creams

Some people make new homes, offices, and other buildings. They make the walls and the roof. Then they put in the doors and windows. It takes a long time to make a building!

Some people make machines. They make the machines in planes, trains, cameras, cell phones, and lots of other things.

Making Planes

Go to pages 26–27 for activities.

 # Helping People

We can help people at home. Parents help children, and young people help old people. These are jobs, but they are not for money.

Some people help lots of people. Doctors and nurses help sick people. Teachers help children at school. Doctors, nurses, and teachers help us all.

A Doctor

A Teacher

What do police officers do? Police officers help people. Firefighters and ambulance workers help people, too. They all help people who are scared, or sick, or in danger. These workers can be in danger when they do their job.

Discover! In Venice in Italy, there are no roads. The firefighters go in boats!

→ Go to pages 28–29 for activities.

6 Jobs with Animals

Lots of people work with animals.

Vets help sick animals. Some vets work on farms, and some vets work in zoos. Some vets work in animal parks. They help wild animals. These vets are helping pandas in an animal park.

Helping Pandas

vets

panda

Some people help animals in danger. These people are washing a pelican. The pelican has oil on its body. The oil comes from a ship.

Washing a Pelican

Some people teach animals to do jobs. They teach guide dogs to help people who can't see. The dogs help the people on busy roads.

Teaching a Guide Dog

Go to pages 30–31 for activities.

Jobs at Night

You sleep at night, but some people do jobs at night! Many doctors and nurses work at night. Some stores and factories are open all night so people have to work there. In the day, people buy lots of food from stores. At night, store workers put more food in the stores.

Working in a Store

tracks

Railway Workers

These railway workers are working on train tracks. They work at night because there are no trains. It's too busy in the day.

Cities are busy at night. People go out to meet friends or to see a movie. When they go home, they can take a taxi. Taxi drivers are busy at night.

Taxi Drivers

Go to pages 32–33 for activities.

8 More Jobs

Do you like singing or dancing?
Do you play music, or do you play
soccer? You can do these things at
school or in your free time. Some
people do these things for a job.
That's how they make money.
These soccer players are working.

Soccer Players

These musicians are working. They are playing instruments. People pay money to watch the musicians.

instruments

Musicians

These people are making a movie. The actors act in the movie. The camera operator uses the camera. The director tells them what to do.

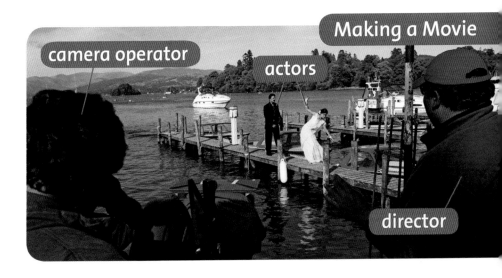

Making a Movie

camera operator

actors

director

There are so many jobs. What job do you want to do?

➜ Go to pages 34–35 for activities.

1 Jobs

← Read pages 4–5.

computer ~~office~~ plane
flight attendant
firefighter   telephone

1 Write the words.

1 __office__   2 _____   3 _____

4 _____   5 _____   6 _____

2 Complete the sentences.

hot   help   ~~are~~   outside   planes

1 Some jobs __are__ inside.

2 Some jobs are _____.

3 Flight attendants work on _____.

4 Flight attendants _____ passengers.

5 Firefighters go into very _____ buildings.

3 Match. Then write the sentences.

People use computers	outside.
Firefighters wear	very hot buildings.
People make roads	in an office.
Flight attendants	a uniform.
Firefighters go into	work on planes.

1 People use computers in an office.

2 _____

3 _____

4 _____

5 _____

4 Circle the odd one out.

1 inside   outside   (orange)

2 computer   body   telephone

3 firefighter   flight attendant   road

4 building   hot   new

5 see   office   go

6 passengers   plane   hot

② In the City

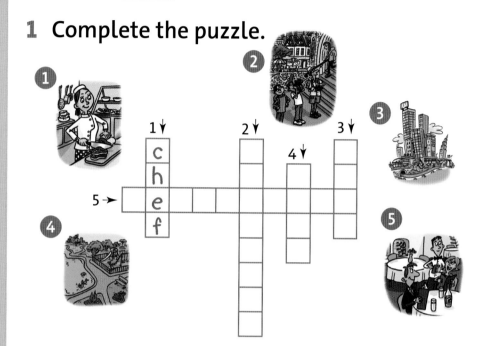

← Read pages 6–7.

1 Complete the puzzle.

```
        1↓           2↓          3↓
        c                        
        h            4↓          
5→      e                        
        f                        
```

2 Write *true* or *false*.

1 Lots of people work in cities.   _true_

2 Chefs work in libraries.   _____

3 Many tourists go to cities.   _____

4 Tour guides help tourists to
cook food.   _____

5 Bus drivers work in cities.   _____

3 Order the words.

1 big / are / and / Cities / busy.

 Cities are big and busy.

2 people / in / Lots of / cities. / work

 _____

3 city. / in a / bus / a / take / can / You

 _____

4 job. / do / a / Bus drivers

 _____

4 Answer the questions.

1 Where do people work in cities?

 People work in stores, parks and
 libraries.

2 What do chefs do?

 _____

3 What do tour guides do?

 _____

4 How can you go from a park to a library?

 _____

3 In the Countryside

← Read pages 8–9.

1 Complete the puzzle. Then write the secret word.

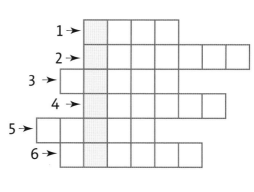

1 →

2 →

3 →

4 →

5 →

6 →

The secret word is:

2 Find and write the words.

ricefishmetalbananascoalolives

1 __rice__   2 _____   3 _____

4 _____   5 _____   6 _____

3 Circle the correct words.

1 In the countryside, many jobs are
  inside / (outside.)

2 Some farmers **grow** / **catch** crops.

3 Some farmers sell **coal** / **animals** at a market.

4 People catch fish from the **store** / **ocean**.

5 Miners find **metal** / **bananas** under the
  ground.

4 Match. Then write the sentences.

Farmers work in	under the ground.
Some farmers	the countryside.
Rice and bananas	keep animals.
Some people catch	are crops.
Miners work	fish from the ocean.

1 _____

2 _____

3 _____

4 _____

5 _____

Making Things

← Read pages 10–11.

cell phone   machine
hands   camera
factory   buildings

1 Write the words.

1 _____

2 _____

3 _____

4 _____

5 _____

6 _____

2 Write *true* or *false*.

1 Lots of people make things.   _____

2 People use their ears to make
    some things.   _____

3 Many people work in factories.   _____

4 People don't use machines in
    factories.   _____

3 Complete the sentences.

> hands people make
> windows new factories

1 Lots of _____ make things.

2 People use their _____ to make some things.

3 People use machines in _____ .

4 Some people make _____ buildings.

5 A building has walls, a roof, doors, and _____ .

6 Some people _____ machines.

4 Order the words.

1 things. / people / make / Lots of

_____

2 work / in / people / factories. / Many

_____

3 a building. / to make / a long time / It takes

_____

4 people / Some / machines. / make

_____

5 Helping People

← Read pages 12–13.

1 Write the words.

1 spenart

parents

2 grande

_____

3 loecpi fieofcr

_____

4 heretac

_____

5 todcor

_____

6 balamunce

_____

2 Circle the correct words.

1 Parents help **doctors** / **children**.

2 **Boats** / **Nurses** help sick people.

3 Teachers **work** / **help** children at school.

4 Ambulance workers help **people** / **roads**.

3 **Match. Then write the sentences.**

Firefighters and Parents help Doctors Teachers help	children at school. help sick people. children at home. ambulance workers help people.

1 _____

2 _____

3 _____

4 _____

4 **Answer the questions.**

1 Who helps sick people?

_____

2 What do teachers do?

_____

3 What do police officers do?

_____

4 Who can be in danger when they do their job?

_____

6 Jobs with Animals

← Read pages 14–15.

1 Find and write the words.

e	t	a	p	z	o	o
b	v	e	t	o	e	t
a	n	i	m	a	l	s
n	e	b	t	s	e	o
a	d	a	n	g	e	r
p	e	l	i	c	a	n

1 zoo _____

2 d _____

3 a _____   4 p _____   5 v _____

2 Complete the sentences.

jobs   sick   dogs   vets

1 Vets help _____ animals.

2 Some _____ work in zoos.

3 People can teach animals to do _____ .

4 Guide _____ help people who can't see.

3 Match. Then write the sentences.

Lots of people	wild animals.
Some vets help	work with animals.
Guide dogs help	animal parks.
Some vets work in	people who can't see.

1 _____

2 _____

3 _____

4 _____

4 Order the words.

1 Some / zoos. / vets / in / work

_____

2 animals / help / danger. / in / people / Some

_____

3 animals / People / teach / jobs. / to do

_____

4 see. / can't / who / people / help / Guide dogs

_____

7 Jobs at Night

← Read pages 16–17.

1 Write the words.

| taxi   train   day   store   night   sleep |

1 _____

2 _____

3 _____

4 _____

5 _____

6 _____

2 Match.

1 You sleep	home in taxis.
2 Many doctors	work on train tracks.
3 Some stores	work at night.
4 Railway workers	busy at night.
5 Cities are	are open all night.
6 People can go	at night.

3 Complete the sentences.

factories   cities   jobs
busy   train   nurses

1 Some people do _____ at night.
2 Many doctors and _____ work at night.
3 Some stores and _____ are open all night.
4 Railway workers work on _____ tracks.
5 In _____ , people go out at night.
6 Taxi drivers are _____ at night.

4 Circle the odd one out.

1 day   food   night
2 movie   nurse   doctor
3 taxi   food   train
4 factory   store   friend
5 busy   meet   see
6 railway   tracks   people
7 sleep   food   night

8 More Jobs

← Read pages 18–19.

1 Write the words. Then match.

1 eviom

___movie___

2 candign

_____

3 creocs

_____

4 snacisumi

_____

2 Write true or false.

1 Soccer players make movies. _____

2 Musicians pay soccer players. _____

3 Musicians play instruments. _____

4 A camera operator acts in a movie. _____

3 **Match. Then write the sentences.**

Some people	in the movie.
The actors act	uses the camera.
The camera operator	people what to do.
The director tells	make movies.

1 _____

2 _____

3 _____

4 _____

4 **Answer the questions.**

1 What do musicians do?

_____

2 Who makes a movie?

_____

3 What do actors do?

_____

4 What job do you want to do?

_____

My Favorite Job

1 What job do you want to do? Think of your favorite job. Complete the diagram.

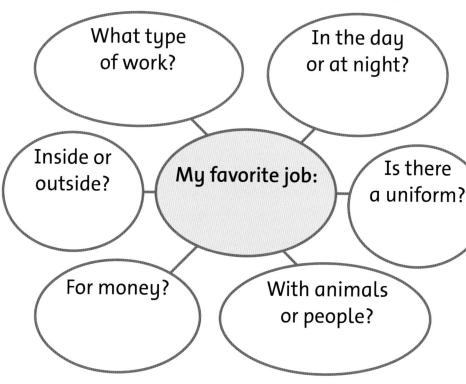

What type of work?

In the day or at night?

Inside or outside?

My favorite job:

Is there a uniform?

For money?

With animals or people?

2 Find or draw a picture of your favorite job.

3 Write about your favorite job.

_____

_____

_____

Job Cards

1 Complete the job cards.

Job	doctor
Place	hospital
When	day or night
Work	help sick people

Job	_____
Place	_____
When	_____
Work	_____

Job	_____
Place	_____
When	_____
Work	_____

Picture Dictionary

 ambulance

 buildings

 buy

 children

 city

 clothes

 coal

 countryside

 crops

 danger

 factory

 food

 gold

 ground

 grow

 machine

 market

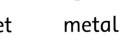 metal

 mine

 money

 ocean

 oil

 parents

 pay

 plane

 protect

 roof

 same

 ship

tourists

 wall

 wild animals

Oxford Read and Discover

Series Editor: Hazel Geatches • CLIL Adviser: John Clegg

Oxford Read and Discover graded readers are at six levels, for students from age 6 and older. They cover many topics within three subject areas, and support English across the curriculum, or Content and Language Integrated Learning (CLIL).

Available for each reader:
- Audio CD Pack (book & audio CD)
- Activity Book

Teaching notes & CLIL guidance: **www.oup.com/elt/teacher/readanddiscover**

Subject Area / Level	The World of Science & Technology	The Natural World	The World of Arts & Social Studies
1 — 300 headwords	• Eyes • Fruit • Trees • Wheels	• At the Beach • In the Sky • Wild Cats • Young Animals	• Art • Schools
2 — 450 headwords	• Electricity • Plastic • Sunny and Rainy • Your Body	• Camouflage • Earth • Farms • In the Mountains	• Cities • Jobs
3 — 600 headwords	• How We Make Products • Sound and Music • Super Structures • Your Five Senses	• Amazing Minibeasts • Animals in the Air • Life in Rainforests • Wonderful Water	• Festivals Around the World • Free Time Around the World
4 — 750 headwords	• All About Plants • How to Stay Healthy • Machines Then and Now • Why We Recycle	• All About Desert Life • All About Ocean Life • Animals at Night • Incredible Earth	• Animals in Art • Wonders of the Past
5 — 900 headwords	• Materials to Products • Medicine Then and Now • Transportation Then and Now • Wild Weather	• All About Islands • Animal Life Cycles • Exploring Our World • Great Migrations	• Homes Around the World • Our World in Art
6 — 1,050 headwords	• Cells and Microbes • Clothes Then and Now • Incredible Energy • Your Amazing Body	• All About Space • Caring for Our Planet • Earth Then and Now • Wonderful Ecosystems	• Food Around the World • Helping Around the World